JOB

OR

BUSINESS:

WHAT NEXT?

By
Oyeleke Olukemi Olubukola

DEDICATION

This book is dedicated to all who desires change in their life.

It's dedicated to you who have made a choice by purchasing this book and ready to apply the knowledge therein.

To you, my inspiration to write the book.

About the Author

Oyeleke Olukemi is an

- o Entrepreneur
- o Project Manager
- o Motivational Speaker
- o Business Engineer
- o Christian
- o Report Writer
- o Blogger
- o Author

She is the Project Manager and founder of Okemscube Multiventures.

Okemscube Multiventures is an ICT company founded in April, 2012 to provide ICT solutions in Bayelsa state, Nigeria and beyond.

She passed out June 2012 with several awards such as being one of the Best Serving Corps Member in Bayelsa state and a 3rd Place winner of NYSC-CBN Venture awards.

You can contact her on
olukemi@okemscube.com

OR

Call +2348053947352

OR www.onlinebiz4real.com

Table of Contents

Copyright 2

DEDICATION 4

About the Author 5

PREFACE 9

Why am I writing this book 10

INTRODUCTION 12

SECTION 1: JOB 16

MODULE 1 16

What is a job? 16

Types of Job 17

Qualifications you need to get a Job......................................18

What other skills are needed? 19

A typical job advert 21

MODULE 2 24

Steps to take in getting a job 24

Prepare a marketable CV 24

Characteristics of marketable CV......................................25

How to write a marketable CV 26

Example of a marketable CV 29

Example of Non-marketable CV 29

Module 3 30

Start submitting your CV's and apply for jobs 30

How to submit your CV Personally 31

Submitting CV's on the internet 31

How to submit your CV through Email application................31

How to submit your CV using Website application................32

How to submit through job websites................33

MODULE 4................33

How to prepare for Aptitude tests................33

Example of online aptitude test question................34

How to Prepare for interviews................35

Preparation for interview 36

Types of questions at interviews or test 37

Results of interview 39

Reasons for rejection 40

NEVER GIVE UP ON YOUR DREAMS 40

JOB APPENDIX................42

1.CV FORMAT GUIDE 42

2. A marketable CV 46

BUSINESS 51

MODULE 1: Business and Entrepreneurship................51

Are you an Entrepreneur? 53

Who is an Entrepreneur?................54

Qualities of successful entrepreneurs 54

MODULE 2:................58

How to start a business................58

Find a niche................59

Register your business 61

Types of company registration 61

How to register your business in Nigeria 62

Conduct a feasibility study................63

Where to now? 67

Who will own the business? 68

MODULE 3...70

How to write a Business Plan...70

Business plan format 70

Develop a Business Strategy 71

How to raise funds for your Business 72

Businesses to start with little capital 73

PREFACE

Job or Business (J.O.B) is a title that have been in my mind since 2012 when as a corps member I was to pass out from service(NYSC)and I was faced with the decision – Job or Business?

It was a question that kept ringing in my head till I was able to pray to God and finally put an answer to it and thank God today am happy doing what am doing.

But a lot of my mates that we went out of the same scheme the same time who did not take time to ask this question till they get an answer are still stuck doing nothing.

Even if it's a job you want, and it's not yet available, you don't need to be idle, cos a popular saying goes that an idle mind is the devil workshop.

Therefore having this book is to help you decide what you will like to do once you are through with either your degree or your service.

And if you are already through and you are still in a dilemma, then this book is good for you.

Why am I writing this book

As an Entrepreneur, Project Manager and Human Resource Personnel of two(2) years, I have discovered that most job seekers that I meet are not prepared for the job they are looking for – they are just looking for job.

Ask them what type of job they are looking for, they will tell you anyone or I don't know. Ask them further, what they will be doing at the job, they will answer anything they give them. And to tell you the truth, that is why a lot of Graduates are still looking for job, because analyses have shown 80% unpreparedness in job seekers.

This book is therefore meant to help you to prepare yourself for a job – if that's what you want.

Or do you want to start a business? How much do you need to start a business? Are there things you need to know before you start your business? Where does a business plan come in? This book will give you all the breakdown information you need regarding a business.

By the time you are through with this book, you must have been convinced that you will start something – either a business or get a job.

INTRODUCTION

Many Graduates Cannot Find Jobs. Despite an Average Economic Growth Rate of About Seven Percent Per Annum Over The Last Seven Years, We Have a Serious Jobless Growth Problem.

Our Economic Performance Over The Last Decade Has Not Translated To Jobs & Real Life Opportunities For Its Many Of Its Youths......World Bank Publication 2012.

As at October, 3rd, 2014 www.tradingeconomics.com have this to say about our economy

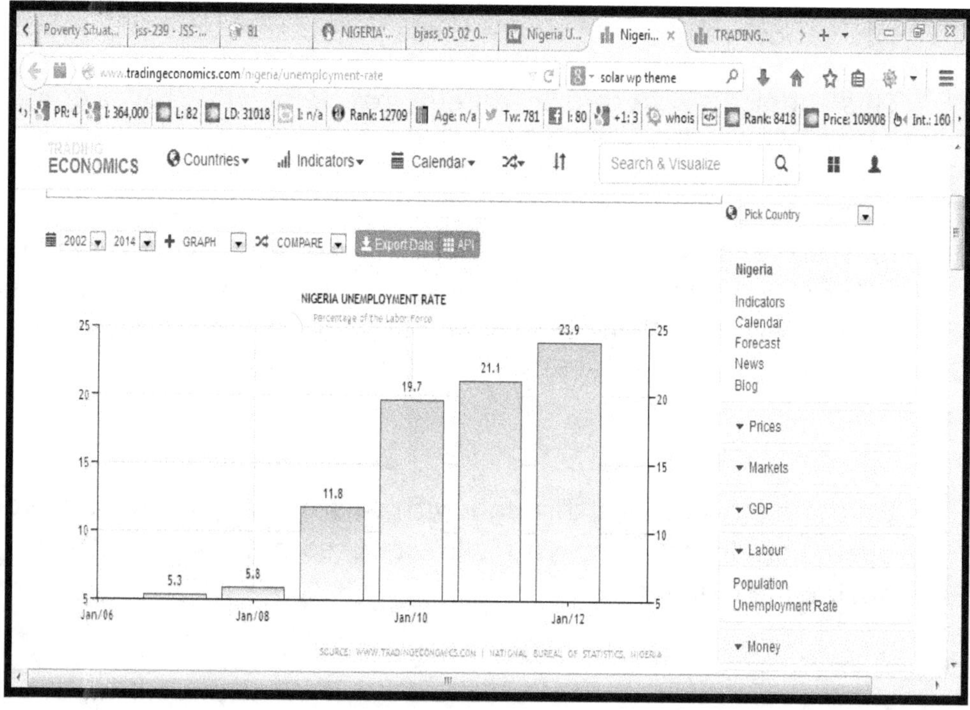

From the chart, Nigeria is said to have 23.9% of unemployment rate.

Dear Compatriots,

You need not panic as there is hope for you.

There's likely to be a lot going on in your Mind right now that with this high level of unemployment, how will I get a job or can I start a business?

You don't need to worry as this book is divided to two parts that talks exclusively on each of this points (Job or Business) conclusively.

As a fresh graduate or a fresh "otondo", you are about to pass out of the NYSC scheme, or you have even passed out, there are 3 important things you need to consider.

I refer to them as three (3) critical milestones. They are:

Milestone 1: Self Exploration

Milestone 2: Location

Milestone 3: Take action

Milestone # 1: SELF EXPLORATION

Many of us are not sure what we specifically want to do immediately after our service but we must take a definite decision on what we want for ourselves?

We need to engage in Self Exploration.

What is self-exploration?

Self-exploration is when you ask yourself very important questions to understand who you are. It is also aimed at you been able to make the JOB or Business decision on time.

Before you ask yourself question, there is somebody supreme you need to consult first, his name is God. He created you with a plan in mind, which you don't know, and so it is very important to ask him questions.

You can ask him:

ASK GOD:

What is my assignment in life?

- Your Assignment Is Like A Ladder Design To Gain Height

What is the purpose of my creation?   What is my Calling?

Let your presence go with me.   Lord show me the way.

Lord show me your glory.

ASK YOUR SELF:

What do I have flair for?   What is my temperament?

What can I do and will enjoy doing whether am paid or not?

What is My Natural Talent?

What is my gift?

- The gift of A man maketh rooms for him, also maketh him stand BEFORE great men. For as you think in your heart, so you are

Milestone#2: Place to stay
Where will you live after service?

- Apartment or Living with Parent?

Living at home -Assuming you still can -- certainly has some advantages: low (or no) rent, home-cooked meals, laundry service, and all utilities included for free.

- Living in an apartment, either by yourself or with some roommates, certainly has its advantages: freedom to do what you want, privacy (up to a point), and a sense you are really an adult because you are living on your own.

Are you going home/staying back?

- Staying Nearby or Moving Away

- Regardless of whether you move back with your parents, stay nearby, or move across the country, you'll need to take decide this on time.

Taking this decision of where to stay to begin your life is a very important one. I would advise that you do it prayerfully as this is the beginning of your destiny.

I have discovered that most times, corps member are in a rush to leave where they serve, when they get home, they meet idleness and they are frustrated and they want to go back to where they have served. Quite unfortunately, by the time they go back, the opportunities that were available as at the time of their passing out are no longer available, and they now have to start hanging around.

I know you will not want this for yourself, so dear, make the decision on time prayerfully.

Milestone #3: take action

- Once you have decided on what to do, start taking actions that will take you there.

- If it's a job, start applying!!!

- If it's a business, write your plan now and start from somewhere.

This book is therfore divided to 2 major sections describing JOB or BUSINESS extensively.

Come along with me

SECTION 1: JOB

MODULE 1

What is a job?

There are several definitions of job. Merriam – Webster dictionary defines job as a piece of work especially; a small miscellaneous piece of work undertaken on order at a stated rate.

Other definition has it as an activity that somebody regularly does for pay

Paid occupation: an activity such as a trade or profession that somebody does regularly for pay, or a paid position doing this.

A motivational speaker once defined job as "positions provided in business". That is, without businesses, jobs cannot be made available. Say for example, the banking business – they employ say 30% of job seekers in Nigeria, if there are no banks, then banking jobs would not have been available. The other type of job we all also clamour for is Oil and gas jobs, but if there are no sustainable oil and gas businesses, the jobs will not be available.

So to be able to get a good paying job, there must be sustainable businesses.

The bottom line in job is that somebody is paying, and this is definitely not the job seeker.

Before you can get a job, you need to be familiar with job environment.

- You need to be able to identify what a job is and the type you are looking for?

- What type of job you really pray for?

- What type of job you will not settle for?

- What qualification do you need?

- What other skills are needed?

Types of Job

Job can be categorized into the following:

- **By time input**: full time and part time job. In advanced countries, most of their jobs pay by the hour, and that is why you see people work 3-4 jobs at the same time.

- **By Proficiency:** skilled and unskilled job. Some job requires level of proficiency – that is capacity to do the work. For example, on a Construction site, jobs that will be available will be for both the skilled like the Architect, Surveyor, Engineer, Artisans (Plumber, Electrician, Iron bender etc.) and also unskilled like the labourers, casual workers etc.

- **By Profession:** this refers to specific disciplines such as Engineering, Medicine, Accounting, Law, etc. To work anywhere as a professional, you must have the prerequisite requirement of the profession. For example, as a Lawyer, you must have been called to the Bar, before you can start practicing.

- **By sector:** also jobs can be categorized by the sector they fall into. Example of such as sales and office jobs, agriculture, mining, construction, manufacturing, and transportation etc.

Qualifications you need to get a Job

To get a job, you need to meet the criteria set for the job. Employers have requirements set for specific positions they are giving out.

General qualifications to note are:

- **Professional qualification**: For you to get professional jobs, you need to be qualified for the job. For example, an Engineer can't apply for a Doctor's job, it's not possible and vice versa.

- **Educational qualification**: Also some jobs require a level of Education standing such the pass-out grade, Post graduate etc.

- **Professional affiliation:** Having a professional certificate is always a plus qualification on any job you want.

- Belonging to association relative to your profession – NBA, NSE, NIM is a plus in some cases and compulsory in some.

- **Years of experience**: Some jobs require that you have previous experience on a similar job. A question that readily comes to my mind when I see 3-5yrs working experience, is where they want fresh graduates to have such? Well, they don't expect graduates to stay idle doing nothing, and that's why I'm imploring you that even if its for free, go and get the working experience.

What other skills are needed?

The world has gone global, and gone are the days you can be boasting of 1st class with no additional skills. Irrespective of what you studied, a universal skill needed for any job now is called **Basic Computer Literacy.** Some people call it **ICT compliant.**

By basic computer literacy – I mean that you need to be able to do at least do the basics on your computer when it comes to a workplace environment. You must be able to at least type, save, print and email documents.

As an HR, I've had reasons to choose a school cert holder over a degree holder because of this.

Let me tell you the story: the new General Manager of an hotel came to our office that they want to recruit new staffs and would like my office to collect CV's and conduct the first interview for them, and that based on our recommendations, they will now do the second interview, and employ.

The vacant positions were Receptionist, Accountant, Supervisor, Laundry man, Caterers, security. We sent out messages and for these 6 positions, we received CV's of not less than 30.

A peculiar case I now had at the interviews was a graduate applying for receptionist post. At the interview, I asked her why she was applying for a job that pay so low, she said she's tired of sitting at home. Ok. The major requirement we have of a receptionist is that she must be able to use excel and the internet well. So I asked her if she can use the computer well, she said not much.

To cut a long story short, we had to employ a school cert who has good computer skills to a graduate holder.

So my dear graduates, you need to equip yourself now for that dream job that you desire. Get the basic computer literacy skill.

Irrespective of the name computer schools call it, the curriculum must cover:

Microsoft Word, Power point, Excel and Internet.

Also Proficiency in IT Skills related to your discipline is very important. e.g. as an Accountant SAGE, EXCEL, PEACH TREE are your IT software packages, Engineers - HYSYS, CISCO, AUTOCAD, MATLAB etc.

Some added skills also value to your résumé such as Project Management Professional(PMP), Health safety and Environment (HSE)

A typical job advert

1. **Graduate Technical Services Engineers Egress Software Technologies Ltd**
Job description

Our Technical Services Engineers play a vital part in the process of turning sales opportunities into longstanding Egress customers. We are looking for talented graduates to fill a number of entry-level opportunities in customer facing technical roles.

Successful candidates will be responsible for supporting the Sales teams growing new business opportunities covering both commercial and government business sectors.

The day to day content of the role varies enormously, but you are likely to:

- Attend pre-sales client meetings and presentations with business development managers
- Determine scope and develop formal proposals
- Identify client requirements: (technical requirements, client infrastructure, configuration, and requirements), technical design (including solution configurations and diagrams) and planning phases of the sales cycle using project management tools and working with partners
- Provide pre and post-sales support for new and existing customers
- Successfully demonstrate products and 3rd Party Solutions in front of prospects
- Work with sales to provide a response for technical RFI/RFP questions
- Participate in all scheduled sales team meetings/conference calls
- Responsibility for the build, delivery and management of proof of concept product evaluations and pilot projects
- Deliver online and onsite product demonstrations (as required or requested)
- Travel, as needed, to industry events, prospect and partner sites
- Develop product training material
- Additional responsibilities include providing on-site support, handling technical presentations at trade shows and conferences; and ensuring proactive communications with customers to ensure customer satisfaction

- For further information about all these opportunities please visit our website.

Qualification and experience requirements

You will either be graduating from University this summer, or a recent graduate looking for your first permanent role or first job change.

You are likely to have chosen a numerate or techncial degree subject (for example Mathematics, Physics, or variants of Computing) and must have a passion for applying those skills in a business environment.

You will possess a natural communication style and outstanding interpersonal skills

Accepted degree subjects

chemical engineering

engineering, electronic and electrical

chemistry

mathematics

computer sciences and IT

physics

engineering, mechanical

How to apply

If you've got what it takes to be successful in these customer facing technical positions and are looking for an opportunity to feel part of something truly inspirational, please get in touch with us now.

Logo: Egress Software Technologies Ltd

Send my CV via email

Apply now

2. Training Associate Recruitment
Nakachi Consulting Ltd

NAKACHI Consulting seeks qualified candidates to fill this role

Responsibilities

- Responsible for marketing NAKACHI training to clients in their State.
- Communicate, Coordinate and Schedule training's for clients in their State.
- Reports to the Membership Co-coordinator on a regular basis.
- Recommend innovative services that can be replicated within the service system.
- Offer frontline NAKACHI Alumni Support within their State.

Qualifications and Requirements

- A university degree in any discipline
- Proficiency in the use of MS Office package and the Social Media.
- Excellent Communication Skills (verbal and written)
- Inter-personal Skills
- Effective and efficient project co-ordination.
- Willingness to travel.
- 1-3 years experience in Marketing

Application Deadline

3 weeks from now

If you see from the two job adverts example, what is needed for an applicant is clearly stated.

Note: Basic use of computer especially (MS- word) was emphasized.

MODULE 2

Steps to take in getting a job

- Prepare a marketable CV.

- Start submitting your CV's and apply for jobs

- Prepare yourself for aptitude tests and interviews- don't stay idle

- Enhance your capacity through learning other skills while waiting

Prepare a marketable CV

What is a CV?

CV stands for curriculum vitae, which means a brief account of your career. CVs are used to explain to recruiters/employers what you can do and what you have done, so a good CV looks forwards as well as accounts for what you did in the past.

A CV should present your knowledge, learning, skills and competencies in a positive, honest way.

It should be arranged in such a way that it will speak for you while you are not there.

An employer/recruiter sees your CV first, and there is a saying that first impression last longer, your CV should leave an indelible impression on the HR perusing your CV.

Therefore your CV should be marketable.

A marketable CV is one that will make employers want to employ you within 30 seconds. There are some CV's that are not marketable.

Please note that, standard HR personnel has just 30 seconds to peruse your CV and so if your cv does not sell itself, it will be discarded.

A marketable CV should include enough information for the HR/recruiter to decide almost immediately that you are likely to be a suitable candidate for the job, and make them call you for the interview.

I would also like to state here that as much having a general CV, it is also good to know the requirements of the jobs you are applying for and use it as a guideline to emphasize those thing they are looking for in the role you are applying for.

An example of such is by showing how you are a good fit by giving examples of how your experience, knowledge and skills fit the requirements of the job, paying particular attention to the ones marked 'essential'.

Characteristics of marketable CV

1. Your details are prominent i.e. name, phone number, addresses and email addresses.

2. Objectives are clearly stated

3. Skills and experiences are listed first

4. Followed by work experience

5. Followed by qualifications

6. Followed by trainings and other certifications

7. Followed by Bio data

8. Followed by hobbies

9. Followed by references

To write a marketable CV is not difficult. It just requires that you try and envision yourself in the pace of an employer and think of why he would like to employ you.

1. Therefore to start, you have your name, phone no, email address and contact address boldly written on top.

2. **Objectives are clearly stated**. Please note very importantly is that the next thing is your career objective NOT your BIODATA.

What is career objective?

Career Objective is what you intend to do with you career as you work in the organization. It also answers the question why do you want to work with the organization. For example an objective can be **"To utilize my skills and proficiencies to solve problems enhance positive change towards the attainment of organizational goals and objectives"**.

3. **Skills and experiences are listed first**: Once you have told an employer why he/she should employ you, the next thing is what Skills you possess that will make you stand out. E.g. Good interpersonal skills, Self -motivated and target oriented, ability to work under pressure etc.

   A point to note here is that don't say what you cannot do.

4. **Followed by work experience:** These skills and experiences you mentioned above, where have you practice them? That's what your working experience answers. It is good to emphasize the role you played in the organisations, especially as it relates to the skills you have.

   Please note that you arrange them in most recent order.

5. **Followed by qualifications:** what qualifications do you have to have worked in the places you have mentioned above. This is also arranged in most recent order.

   It is important to note here that it not advisable to write 20XX-20XY when indicating the year if you didn't graduate normally/on time from your school because at the time the HR is looking at your CV, you won't be there to explain why. At such times, just mention the year you graduated, that's all.

6. **Followed by trainings and other certifications:** This part explains your professional skills earlier mentioned, how and where you got them?

7. **Followed by Bio data:** Yes, it is now safe here to talk about you because now you have piqued the HR interest to want to know who is this skillful hand that I can employ.

8. **Followed by hobbies:** in listing your hobbies, please be conscious of the job you are applying for. Say for example, you are aplplying for the post of a confidential secretary, and in y

9. **Followed by references**: Your references are not supposed to be your family members. They are expected people of reputation that can verify you as a person.

   Depending on the job you are applying for, you can include your references or state it there that it's available on request.

Two typical examples of CV are compared in the next page. On the first CV, you will see that the writer includes that he is self-motivated and target oriented. Already if he's looking for a marketing job, with those criteria, he is already qualified.

The second cv- non marketable one, was just filled with bio data and no useful information at first glance.

Example of a marketable CV

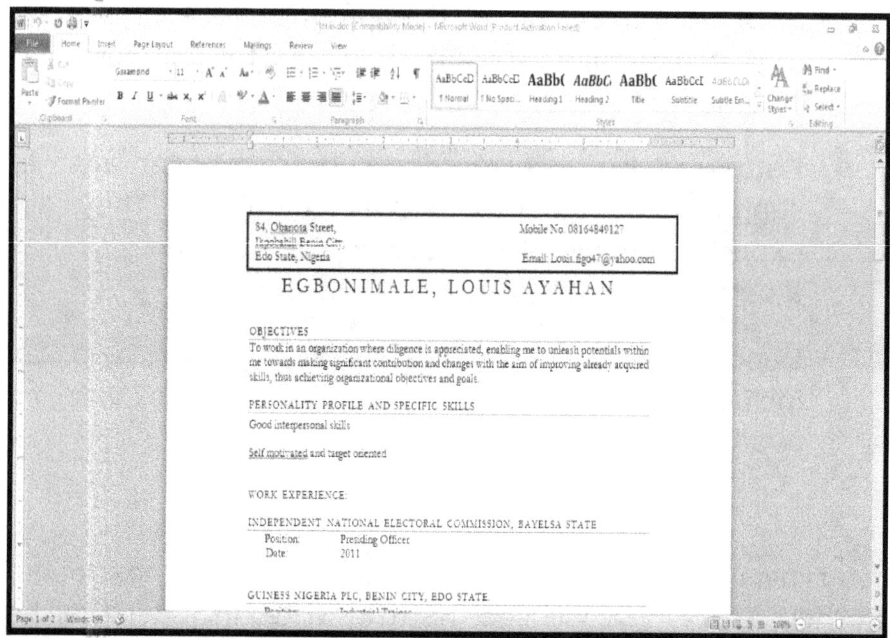

Example of Non-marketable CV

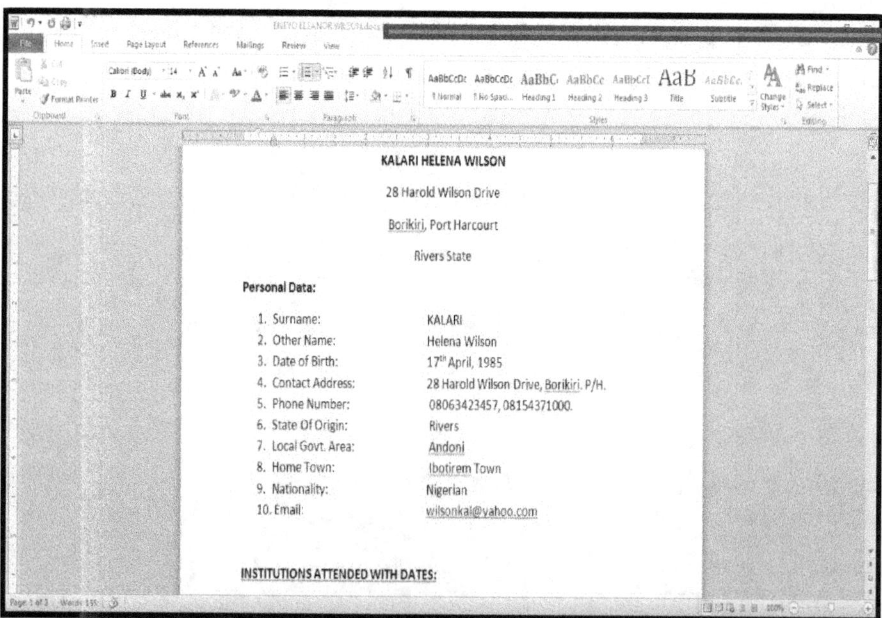

Please note:

- o **CV are not meant to be generic – that it is, you must edit your CV to suit the job you are applying for.**

- o **Be aware of the criteria of the job before preparing your CV**
- o **Emphasize these criteria.**

Module 3

Start submitting your CV's and apply for jobs

Now that you have a marketable CV, it's time to start applying for jobs. As an applicant/ job seeker, follow up on job adverts in the dailies, on job websites and apply to relevant organizations.

There is need for you to learn how to submit your CV yourself on the internet.

Applying for job these days is majorly done in 4 ways

1. Personal submission of CV
2. Email application
3. Internet application
4. Submission through job websites

How to submit your CV Personally

Some job adverts always indicate apply in person if interested in a specific job. To do this as a job seeker:

- Make enquiries about the job posted
- Go along to the company with your marketable CV
- You can write an application letter alongside your marketable cv, but this is not ccompulsory.

- Go the company properly dressed. I'm emphasizing proper dressing here because some companies conduct interview immediately.

Submitting CV's on the internet

submitting CV's on the internet is of 3 types

1. Email application
2. Website application
3. Job websites

How to submit your CV through Email application

Some job post require that you send email to a particular email to show your interest. To do this, it is of the advantage if you have a functional email address.

A functional email address is one you have access to, and you check often, not the one you can't remember the password or other details.

To submit your cv via email, do the following:

- Type your CV in word document: I'm surprised sometimes to receive CV's in picture formats from applicants. This is wrong. You should prepare your CV in word format and at most convert it to a printable document format(pdf).
- After typing your CV in word document, open your email and click on compose.
- **Subject of mail:** Some are specific about the subject of the mail, some are not. Nevertheless it is good to give your mail a good subject e.g. Adesare Adegbagi's CV for the post of the Admin manager.
- **Body of mail:** Kindly find attached my CV. Thanks. Name, signature
- Then attach your CV in the mail and click on send.

Please note that it is always good to use your personal email address for such applications as further correspondences will be replied to any mail you use.

How to submit your CV using Website application

This requires you to go to the website of the company to upload your CV and relevant materials.

It is important to note here that, your activities on social media can be a plus or minus for you here.

Some company only uses your social media login as an access to their application portal. So be watchful and careful of your post on social media networks.

To submit your CV on a particular website, just go the website and follow the set requirements. For example if you want to apply to shell, you will have to go online using the following steps:

1. Type the website address in the address bar e.g www.shell.com
2. Then go to the option, job and careers http://www.shell.com/global/aboutshell/careers.html
3. click on, click here to create a new account.
4. An agreement page opens , and you click on agree
5. You will be required to put your email and security questions and answers
6. Click on submit.

I would like to note that if you have not prepared for aptitude tests, do no do shell applications, as they will require you write an aptitude test within 7 days of applying.

How to submit through job websites

There are job websites online. Sign upon the sites and upload your CV's.

Some of the sites are:

www.hotnigerianjobs.com
www.jobberman.com

www.jobrapido.com.ng
www.nigeriabestjobs.com

MODULE 4

How to prepare for Aptitude tests

Some companies do test first, then interview.

While some do it simultaneously depending on their organization structure.

Some people once they submit their CV will relax and start watching season movies, frolicking with friends and jollying around. Yes they are all good but they need to be done at the right time.

After you've submitted your CV, start preparing for aptitude test by reading GMAT and relevant materials.

- Practice questions daily

- Research more about companies that you have applied to.

- If possible, apply to graduate training schools

In the case of Shell, your aptitude start within 7 days and you are required to pass a stage before you proceed to the next stage. If you are successful overall, you will be invited for an interview.

Aptitude test varies depending on the company.

Example of online aptitude test question

Multiple oil companies operate at one Shell facility, each producing thousands of barrels of oil per day. Your team measures the production from each company to provide a weekly report. Individual companies also keep their own records. Recently, one company reported concerns that your last reading was lower than theirs by 200 barrels. What do you do?

1. Counterproductive 2. Ineffective 3. Neutral   4. Effective   5. Highly Effective

	Not rated	1	2	3	4	5
Most	Least					

A.   Ask your team to conduct the measurements for that company twice this week to double check the results before you produce the report.

B.   Find out what method the other company uses to take the measurement. Repeat the test using their method to see if you get the same results.

C.   Ask the other companies if your results are accurate. If so, explain to the company who is complaining that it must be their measurement which is inaccurate.

D.   Speak to your colleagues in the operations team to find out if there were any circumstances at the time which may have affected the results of the measurements.

If you purchase this book, your email have been registered and a link to aptitude test and GMAT is will be sent to you. Check your email for details. If you are reading a friends copy, purchase your own on www.joborbusiness.com

How to Prepare for interviews

- An interview is a structured meeting between you and your employer.

- An interview is an opportunity for you to market yourself.

- Joseph was for an interpreter job but through his preparedness he got a Prime Minister job – a post that did not exist before

Types of interview

- Phone interview

- One-one interview

- Group/panel

- Social/meal

- Site interview/ visit

- Gouram – take place like reality shows

- Internship

Preparation for interview

1. Know the company & position – from internet

- Know yourself

- What are your skills

2. Practice – Dry run

3. Be prepared, use your friends as practice

4. Dress well

5. The gift of a man makes way for him. What is your gift?

At the interview

1. Be time conscious

- Arrive early

- Be polite and friendly

- Respond appropriately

2. Understand the culture

- Eye contact, mannerism and composure

- Do not fidget

What should you take for an interview?

- A pen and a good notepad

- Original copies of your certificates

- A copy of your CV. Why? You may have updated your CV and they may not have seen it.

Stages at the interview

- Introduction - the interviewer wants to get to have what is known as first impression

- Invitation: review of CV

- Discussion: opportunities in the company

- Close out: clarification

Types of questions at interviews or test

1. Most test questions or interviews are Behaviour based questions.

In this kind of question, they will set scenario for you to answer what is the most appropriate response.

How to answer behaviour based question

To answer this type of question, use the acronym STAR

- Situation – understand the situation been described.

- Task – what exactly is the task required?

- Action – what action do you need to take?

- Result – what is the result to achieve? From the situation and definition of task at hand, you must have been able to take the appropriate action to give you the desired result.

2. What can you contribute to our establishment?
Every employer wants to employ an asset and not a liability. You therefore need to convince the interviews you are worth the investment. You mention your strengths and what you think you can do better.

3. What does the course you have studied impacted on you?
You should be able to relate knowledge gained to practical knowledge.

4. Tell us about your IT experience.
You are to share skills gained on IT here and any other worthwhile experience that you gained that will help you on the job.

5. What are your strengths?
Emphasize the strengths that is beneficial on the job.

6. What are your weaknesses?

Do not down play your weaknesses, and make it clear to them you are working on it. Do not list it too much.

7. How much do you think we should pay you.
A very daisy question.

Answer: With my contribution to the company, pay me what is commensurate to my effort.

Or

Pay me according to the salary scheme of the company.

8. Tell us more about yourself.
Here, do not talk too much. Emphasize your strength always.

Type of behaviour based question

- Decision making

- Problem solving

- Analytical

- Creativity

- Risk taking

- Leadership

- Management

- Empathy

- Visioning

- Feedback

- Assertiveness

- Organisation and planning

Results of interview

- Now that you are through with the test, it's either you pass or fail.

- You may pass and still be rejected for other reasons.

- Anyways, DO NOT be too hard on yourself when you are not employed.

- It's not the end of the world and don't make people around you miserable for that.

Reasons for rejection

- Poor communication

- Poor personal appearance

- Uncertainty

- Lack of enthusiasm or interest in the job

- Excessive interest in benefits, pays and packs

- Lack of knowledge about the organisation

- Lack of confidence or overconfidence

- Lack of integrity, Excessiveness and Dishonesty

- Organisation changes and uncertainties

- Lack of skill required

<u>**What Next?**</u>

- Keep trying until you will get that dream job don't QUIT.

- Quitters never win and WINNERS never quit.

- Which one are you?

NEVER GIVE UP ON YOUR DREAMS

Volunteering

- Volunteering after NYSC can be a great way to develop valuable skills and experience.

- Demonstrating these skills to potential employers can give you a competitive edge when it comes to building your career, there are thousands of volunteering opportunities available and so you're bound to find one that interests you.

- You could choose to volunteer part-time for a few days, or apply for a full-time volunteering placement in Nigeria or overseas.

JOB APPENDIX

1.CV FORMAT GUIDE

NAME:

....
....

ADDRESS:

....
....
....

TELEPHONE NOS:

....
....

EMAIL ADDRESS:

....
....

CAREER OBJECTIVES:

....
....
....
....
....
....

SKILLS YOU HAVE:

....
....
....
....
....
....

YOUR PERSONALITY PROFILE:

....
....

....
....
....
....

WORKING EXPERIENCE:
NYSC
PPA..
....
Post:..
....
....
Others
   1. Name Of Establishment:

....
....
      Post..
....
      Year..
....

   2. Name Of Establishment:

....
....
      Post..
....
      Year..
....

   3. Name Of Establishment:

....
....
      Post..
....
      Year..
....

EDUCATION
   1. Tertiary

Name of school:

.... Year ....

Course:

....

Name of school:

.... Year ....

Course:

....
....

2. Secondary School: ....
    Year ....

3. Primary School: ....
    Year ....

BIO DATA:
State of Origin:

....

L.G.A:

....
....

Sex:

....
....

Date of Birth:

....

Marital Status:

....

Religion:

....
...

Language Spoken:

....

Hobbies:

....
.....

REFEREES:

1. NAME:...
....
PHONE
NO...
....
ADDRESS:
....
.....

2. NAME:...
....
PHONE
NO...
....

ADDRESS:
....

This format was used to prepare this CV and the guy got a job just 2 months after passing out. You can call him to verify.

He's one of the people who had been at my lectures and made use of it.

If you don't know how to arrange your CV, you call us at Okemscube to help you.

KABOWEI MAXWELL OYINKURO

Close 55 House 1A, Satelite Town, off Badagry Expressway, Finiger Bus-stop, Ojo.Lagos State.

Email:oyenskabon@yahoo.com. **Phone No.:** 08138177700, 08053068720

CAREER OBJECTIVE: To utilize my skills and proficiencies to solve problems enhance positive change towards the attainment of organizational goals and objectives

SKILLS

- Computer literate (MS Word ,MS Excel etc.)
- Good oral and written communication skills
- Excellent interpersonal & entrepreneurial skills
- Attention to detail, able to work under pressure
- Excellent team player and ability to work independently with minimal supervision

SUMMARY OF EDUCATION

2008- 2012   Lagos State University, Ojo, Lagos State

B.Sc (Business Administration) Second Class Honours

1998 -2002   Ojoku High School, Tolu Complex, Ajegunle

Lagos State (SSCE)

1992 – 1997   Local Authority Primary School, Ajegunle. Lagos

First School Leaving Certificate (FSLC)

PROFESSIONAL CERTIFICATES

- 2014   Member,Nigeria Institute of Management (NIM)
- 2014   Proficiency Certificatein Management (PCM)
- 2014   Institute of Safety Professionals of Nigeria(ISPON) General HSE Certificate
- 2014 Institute of Safety Professionals of Nigeria (ISPON) HSE Supervision (Level 3) Certificate.

WORKING EXPERIENCE

May 2014- Till Date   First City Monument Bank

Direct Sales Representative (DSA)   Yenagoa, Bayelsa State

April 2013 –Feb. 2014 (NYSC)   **MINISTRY OF EDUCATION**

Unified Examination Schedule Officer   Yenagoa, Bayelsa State

Job Description

- Collection of data from schools for registration
- Conducting and monitoring primary School examination.
- Issuing of First School Leaving Certificate.

July 2006 – October 2010   **PROMASIDOR NIGERIA LTD.**

Machine Operator   *3a&bCowbell   wayIsolo   Industrial,Estate, Isolo, Lagos State.*

Job Description

- Ensuring smooth running of production machines to meet organizations production target.
- General maintenance and installation of production machines..

BIO DATA

State of Origin: Bayelsa State

L.G.A.:   Sagbama

Sex: Male

Date of Birth: 17th October, 1988

Marital Status: Single

Nationality: Nigerian

Language Spoken: English, Ijaw and Yoruba

REFERENCES

Mr. Brown Ebikene

Central Bank of Nigeria

Senior Manager.

Other Banking Institution Department

Enugu State

Tel: 080332000000,

Mr. Epegu Kins Menidin

Chief Education Officer

Ministry of Education

Yenagoa,

Bayelsa State.

Tel:0803790000000

BUSINESS

MODULE 1: Business and Entrepreneurship

<u>Introduction</u>

Having discussed elaborately on Job, the truth of the situation in Nigeria is that we need sustainable businesses for jobs to be available.

Businesses operate in a chain reaction. Take for example, my experience in ICT business. I had a contract for supplying computers and deploying Internet in a location. For that contract, I employed two(2) engineers, bought computers in a computer shop, fuel the generator, paid on ISP and deliver the project.

At the end of the project, I then realised how much we are losing as a country when we send out our money by buying imported product because all the chains in the production link that will benefit us as Nigerians have been taken out.

I believe that is why Nigeria as a whole now is stressing business and skills development as a panacea to job creation.

This part of the book is therefore dedicated to all those who would like to start a business and get it right from the beginning.

Starting a business is not as difficult as sustaining a business.

The most important thing to consider, when thinking of starting a business is the sustainability. How will the business fare in the long run?

What is Business?

Business is a commercial or mercantile activity engaged in as a means of livelihood. Also, business can be defined as solutions to other people's problem.

Therefore for you to start a business, you must find solution to people's problems.

Why do you want to start a business?

In order for your business to be sustainable and pass the tides of life and time, you need to recognize from the onset, why you are starting the business.

If the business do not have a major reason for it, or the main reason is to make ends meet, when you have been able to make ends meet, you will then forget that your business needs to be sustained and retain, and your business will come crashing. I know you don't want this, and so from the onset, get your priorities right .... Why do you want to start a business?

Don't forget the no. 3 of our critical milestone which is "Take action".

In this part of the book, your action will be a lot of writing and jotting.

Reasons why people start businesses

People start businesses for different reasons. Some are listed below:
- To make profit.
- To provide a service to the community.

- To improve the loving standard of your family.
- To be your own boss.
- For a change.
- For contact with people.
- For pleasure.

There are more and they are not generic. They are peculiar to individuals and businesses.

> **Action 1**: *Write down five reasons why you want to start a business?*

Are you an Entrepreneur?

Now that you know why you want to start a business, the other big question is "Are you an Entrepreneur"?

This is very important because it is the entrepreneurial spirit God has deposited in you that will keep you going when the going gets tough.

To know if you are really an entrepreneur, ask yourself these questions:

- Are you hardworking?
- Do you like providing solutions?
- Do you like dealing with people?
- Are you reliable?
- Are you good at giving directions?
- Can you make decisions quickly?
- Do you know enough about the product or service you are about to sell?
- Do you have the time needed to operate and organise your business?

If you answer "no" to more than two of these, you will have to change your outlook to become a successful entrepreneur and for your business to succeed.

<u>**Who is an Entrepreneur?**</u>

An entrepreneur is a person who organises, controls, runs and owns a business venture or commercial undertaking involving risks. Risk; in a business venture, generally involve the probability of loss of capital investment and/or profit. It is the task of every entrepreneurs to reduce the probability of loss and infact to increase "reasonable" profit.

Entrepreneur is one who organizes, manages and **assumes** the risk of a business entreprise.

The greatest task of an Entrepreneur is the assumption of the risk. This is what differentiates the Employees and an Entrepreneur. If the business collapses, the employees will look for another job, while the Entrepreneur will bear the loss majorly.

It is therefore the constant work of the Entrepreneur to remain innovative, and to be ahead in the field to keep the business rolling and sustainable.

<u>Qualities of successful entrepreneurs</u>

Vision	Leadership	Chance	Passion
Strategic Thinking	Energy	Follow through	Discernment of time
Creativity	Problem solving	Time management	Ever ready to ask for help
Negotiation skills	Perseverance	Confidence	The ability to produce results
Alertness	Resilience	Self-urgency	Ability to take calculated risk

| Assertiveness | Be a self-starter | Always learning | Has a winning mindset |

Action 2: Write down the personal traits which would help make you a Successful entrepreneur (at least five).

What do you need to start a business?

Is it idea or money?

Many atimes, at presentations, people tell me that their major challenge in starting their business is money – I always disagree.

In as much as I would have loved to agree, experience and case studies have shown that **a feasible business Idea** is what you need to start a business.

Ideas that provides solutions to people's problem is the major requirement to people's problem.

Money/capital is needed to finance a business, but without an idea that is well formed, articulated, written down and turned in a business plan, which is then followed as a blueprint to run the business, the money will be wasted.

As a young person, a lot of ideas may be running through your mind, but to start a business you need to:

1. Itemize and document the ideas: this does not have to be in any order, but it's important as an Entrepreneur to have a book of ideas where you write the ideas as it comes to you. It could be a handy jotter, your noepad on pc, or your diary.

2. Check the ideas – are they viable?

3. Arrange the ideas in the order of viability.

4. Develop the most viable idea and conduct a feasibility study.

5. Prepare a business plan: Once it is proven from the feasibility study that business is feasible and sustainable, you can now go ahead to do a business plan.

Starting a business: are you making the right decisions

As a new Entrepreneur, there are times on your entrepreneurial journey that you will keep asking yourself if you are making the right decisions, sometimes it will seem that you should just turn back, forget about the business and look for a job, irrespective of the pay, you feel like giving up.

Don't give up!!!

It is very important, so that you can accomplish your dreams of starting the business.

At the onset of your business decision, 2 major criteria for you to consider are:

1. The God factor
2. The you factor

The God Factor

- Have you ever ask God for your purpose in life?
- The business you are about to embark on, will it suit God's purpose for your life?
- What line of work will suit God's purpose for your life?
- Describe what your purpose in life is?
- Does it tally with the business you want to run?

- Is it a business that will make you fulfill your purpose?
- Can you feel God's hand leading you in your idea?

No matter how good an idea is, without God it cannot materialize.

The You factor

- Who are you?
- What do you know about yourself?
- What do you know about entrepreneurship?
- How many of the required characteristics of an entrepreneur do you have?
- Are you willing to pay the price of entrepreneurship?
- What business are you passionate about?

Entrepreneurship comes with a price. So before you think of venturing into a business, you have to weigh carefully the price of setting up a business in terms of personal costs. Setting up and running a business drains both your time and your energy levels.

As an Entrepreneur just starting your business, it will consume your time, energy and money. You will likely experience some of the points listed below:

- Less time with your children.
- Less time for socialising and community duties.
- Less energy for family responsibilities.
- Absences from home and community to handle business situations.
- Your funds are tied up in the business.
- Less sleep.

Once your business is up and running, and functioning well, you will now enjoy.
- ❖ You will be your own boss, and you don't have to rely on anybody

- ❖ You will determine your pay
- ❖ You will have flexibility in the hours and mode of work
- ❖ You will not need to look for job as job will be looking for you – do you know that some company will want to poach you from your business when they see how well you run it.
- ❖ You will have the possibility to earn more money as your business grows
- ❖ You also have the possibility that your business will grow in the future.

Running a business is an exciting and rewarding venture, if proper planning and follow through is done.

Action 3: *Write down 5 things that will motivate you to continue in your business when the going gets tough.*

MODULE 2:

<u>How to start a business</u>

1. Find a niche.

2. Find a problem your niche is facing and provide a solution.

3. Conduct a feasibility study.

4. Register your business.

5. Write a business plan – develop a strategy to market you solution to your niche.

6. Start your business.

7. Follow through your business plan and optimize as you go.

<u>Find a niche</u>

Every business sector has niches in them. It is therefore important that as an Entrepreneur that you recognize your niche.

What is a niche?

A niche is a place, employment, status for which a person or thing is best fitted.

A niche is an area that comes naturally to you. It is the business you will do passionately with or with Every sector have niches. It is therefore up to you as an entrepreneur to find your niche. For example in the entertainment sector, there is movies, singing, drama, fashion niches and each of them can still be broken down as much as it can be.

The key thing for you to note when choosing a niche is that is has the capacity to fund your business. You can also look at your niche from a customer's perspective – do you have enough customers in your niche who will sustain your business?

How do find your niche

1. By praying.
2.   Identifying personality and temperament.
3. Primary profession and training.
4. Exploring a skill learnt.
5. Expanding a skill learnt.

Niche is an habitat where you are passionate about. In you niche, you are willing to learn and grow your business.

Identifying personality and temperament

As an entrepreneur, this is key for you when identifying your niche, because it will determine the sustainability of your business in the long run. Also, identifying your temperament gives you an idea of the kind of people you need to employ in your business.

Four Basic Temperament Chart

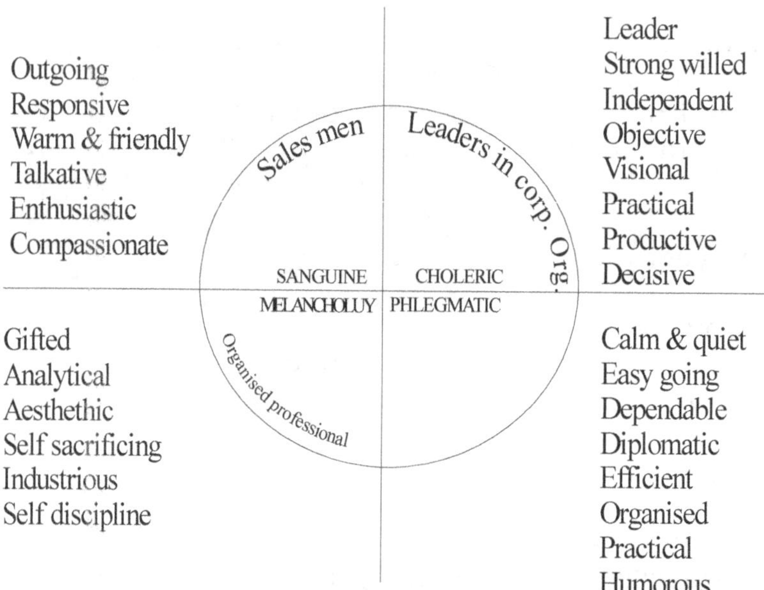

A typical example of using this chart is if you are a sanguine, you know that you should not run a business that will not make you meet people rather your business should be people oriented.

Register your business

The next thing for you to do once you identify your niche is to register your business. Why I suggest this before writing your business plan, is that it will give you facts you can rely on when you are writing your plan. By the time you register your business, you are already committing yourself to make your business succeed.

Legislation and other statutory registration will come later.

Types of company registration

In Nigeria today, there are three (3) types of company registration in CAC namely:

- Enterprise or business name (small scale business) minimum of one (1) person.
- Limited liability Company (Minimum of two; maximum of fifty).
- Public limited liability Company.

The major differences in the three is that enterprise do not have liabilities or shareholders, and so the business liability is in the name of the owner.

As a beginner, depending on your type of business, you can at least register a business name, then upgrade it as your business expands.

Certification

If your business is a specialized business such as manufacturing, building, production, etc. You need to get certification from statutory relevant authorities/regulatory bodies such as SON, ICAN, COREN, NSE, NAFDAC, CPN, PMI, NISP ...

Therefore, you should make enquiry of their cost and include it in your business plan. Once you commence business, ensure that you fill and pay the fees necessary, so that these bodies will not disrupt your business and organisations.

How to register your business in Nigeria

- Go to any CAC office located in all state capital and Abuja.
- Obtain business name search form, it is just N500.
- Fill and submit the form.

- After two weeks, go and check if you name is available, if it is, ensure that you register within sixty days.

For people that have already registered business name and not running a business.

- Kindly note that your annual filing return is increasing every year and it at the end of ten years, you didn't file your annual returns, they will delete your name in the directory.

Conduct a feasibility study

A feasibility study is a research you make to know it your business will be feasible. Feasibility shows whether it will make money or not.

Is your business feasible?
Before deciding whether to start a particular business or not, you should determine whether the business will be feasible, in other words whether it would make money or not.

Basically, there are six steps towards determining the feasibility of your business:
- ✓ Step 1 Choose a product or service to sell
- ✓ Step 2 Find out if people will buy the product or service
- ✓ Step 3 Decide how your business will operate
- ✓ Step 4 Estimate how much it will cost you to operate your business
- ✓ Step 5 Estimate how much you will make from sales
- ✓ Step 6 Compare your expected income and your expected costs

STEP 1: Choose a product or service to sell
There are a number of questions you should ask yourself in deciding what sort of business you should establish and where you should set it up.

- Is there a demand for the product?
- Look and see what businesses there are in your community now. What products do people need?
- Are there already businesses that provide these things?
- What are some products or services that are not available in your community?
- How many similar businesses are already in operation?
- If there are already several other businesses in operation which provide the same product or service you want to, your business may not be feasible.
- It depends whether what you offer will be unique in some way (cheaper, better, special, etc.).
- What skills do you possess to run your business?

You should know enough about your business to offer a good product or provide good services.
Otherwise you may have to either get training in that area or choose another product or service you do know.

- What benefits do you wish to gain from running your business?

Apart from making a profit, you may wish to gain pride in yourself, help create new jobs, improve your status in the community or even provide products or services which you see as necessary.

STEP 2: Will people want to buy your product or service?
How can you find out if people will pay for your product or service? Or, in business language, is there a market for your product? In particular, if what you sell is new or unique, you have to be able to answer certain questions to see if your business is a good idea or not.

- Is there a demand for your product or service?

- Where should your business be located to attract the most customers?
- How much competition do you have?
- How many potential customers do you have?
- What is a suitable price you can ask for your product?

To find out if people will buy your product you should:
- Visit a market or a store and observe what similar products customers buy
- Find out what people have in their homes that is related to your product or service
- Talk to people who are already selling a similar item
- Set up a 'focus group interview'

A 'focus group interview' is a useful tool for finding out why customers might or might not buy your product or service. Very simply, you bring together a small number of people who represent a cross-section of the potential customers you have identified.

The interviewer (usually you) asks the members of the group direct questions about the advantages and disadvantages of a product or service. Asking the group what they think of competitors' products or service can also give you an insight into what mistakes not to make or how you can make your own business unique.

STEP 3: Decide how your business will operate
A number of questions must be considered such as:
• What is involved in the production process from start to finish?
• How long does the production cycle take?
• What resources do you need to run your business (transportation, raw materials, start-up money, etc.) and where can you get them?
• What skills do you need and how will you learn them?
• Will you need to hire employees?

STEP 4: Estimate how much it will cost you to operate your business

Make a list of all of your planned expenses for each month such as:

- salaries
- raw materials
- rent
- electricity
- advertising
- water
- insurance

office supplies
tools
 fuel
maintenance
 packaging
transport
bank charges

Estimate the monthly costs for these expenses.

Add any other monthly expenses which you know about – although each month might differ owing to seasonal trends, you should be able to estimate an average month's expenses.

Exercise note: Enter the monthly cost estimates for your proposed business onto a spreadsheet.

STEP 5: Estimate how much you will make from sales

After talking to potential customers and observing people who are purchasing or using a product or service similar to yours, you should have an idea of how much you can sell in one month. The price of your product should also be considered.

After you have determined your total operating costs of doing business, you'll be ready to plan what you will have to add to the cost of your products to set profitable selling prices.

Some factors that will affect your decision on pricing are:

- shipping costs
- your competitors' pricing
- operating costs
- your customers' need or desire for your product
- your customers' image of the value of your product or service

Once you have set prices for your product or service, you can then prepare a sales estimate. To estimate your monthly sales, simply multiply the number of sales you expect to make in one month times the average price you will be asking for your product or service.

Exercise note: Enter your estimated sales onto the spreadsheet.

STEP 6: Compare expected income and expected costs

Subtract your expected costs from your expected income to see if your average month will show a profit. You will also need to estimate the costs involved with starting your business, e.g. purchasing equipment, supplies, setting up a shop or work area, etc.

These start-up costs will obviously have to be paid out before you even start making an income.

If you have estimated conservatively for sales but estimated slightly higher than you think for costs, you should have a good idea of whether your business will be feasible.

If your costs are more than your sales, you'll have to look again at how to make the business feasible. This might involve deciding on a way of reducing your costs or somehow increasing your sales.

Where to now?

If you've shown on paper that your business is feasible, ask yourself, 'Now, what do I do?' If your family or friends have plenty of money that they are willing to pour into your business venture, this question is already answered. But for those of you who will have to find the money to start up your business, you may have to get assistance – both in getting the money and for advice on setting up the business.

Who will own the business?

Basically, there are three main styles of operation your business can take.

These are:

1. Sole owner (self-owned)
2. Partnership (owned by more than one person)
3. Company (owned by shareholders)

SOLE PROPRIETORSHIP

Sole owner means simply that you own your company by yourself. Even if you have a loan from a bank or a friend or family member, a sole owner is a legal classification which determines the way your business will operate.

Advantages	Disadvantages
You are your own boss	All the responsibility is on your shoulders
You can keep in touch with all sides of the business	The owner is responsible for all the debts quickly of the business
Decisions can be made quickly	You are probably unable to put in as much money

PARTNERSHIP

Partnership means that you own the business jointly with at least one other person. These partners must enter into an agreement or contract if the partnership is to continue for more than a year.

Advantages	Disadvantages
The extra capital means the business can expand more rapidly	A partner may be committed to debts incurred by another partner
Each partner can handle one aspect of the business at times	Shared management can be trying

If a partner is ill, the other(s) can carry on	Disputes can arise regarding the time & effort put in by each partner

It is usually advisable for a lawyer to draw up the necessary contract. This helps prevent any legal difficulties later. The contract should clearly state all of the important terms of the partnership.

The contract usually contains the following information:
– Who the partners are
– The purpose of the partnership
– The duration of the partnership
– The amount invested by each partner
– The duties of each partner
– Special provisions with salaries, profits, etc.

Remember to add the cost of legal fees into your start-up costs if you do use a lawyer's services to prepare a contract.

A Company is usually set up for larger businesses and involves shareholders and boards of directors. Many small businesses will likely operate as either a sole owner or a partnership.

Advantages	Disadvantages
More money is available to set up the business	You are sharing management of the company with all the shareholders
Your shareholders can help in getting customers	Your shareholders can block your Decisions

MODULE 3

How to write a Business Plan

If you have a good idea in your head, without you writing it down in form of a plan, it cannot come to pass. Writing your ideas down in form of a plan, especially a business plan is what makes your conceptualize your idea from start to finish.

You need a business plan.

A business plan is to show potential investors that is your business is feasible and profitable and that you have a plan on how to run it.

Business plan format

Business plan have the same essential makeup. It only have slight variations depending on the audience you want to address or send it to.

By God's grace I've written business plan to CBN (won 2nd place 2011/12 Batch for NYSC – CBN awards), written for clients to Bank of Agriculture(BOA), also for a client for shell live wire programme and numerous others.

In all these business plans, their structure is the same, the major difference most of the time is

- The cover page.
- Some lexical words e.g. some use marketing plan while some would say marketing strategy.
- The required capital.

If you have an access to one million naira, you will not write a plan for ten million naira capital.

General format of a business plan

- Cover page
- Executive summary
    - Introduction
    - Product/services
    - Marketing plan summary
    - Competitor analysis summary
    - Management team overview
    - Financial summary
- Company summary
- Description of the business
- Products and services
- Market analysis
- Competitor analysis
- Marketing plan
- Operational plan
- Financial plan
- Conclusion
- Appendix

Develop a Business Strategy

It is advisable that you prepare your business plan yourself to give you the know-how of running your business from the onset.

You can use your business plan to raise loan, sponsorship, win grants like the NYSC-CBN venture award, Youwin . . .

Your business plan must include

- Executive summary

- Product description

- Market analysis

- Marketing...

Start something!!!

- The major challenge you may likely face now is capital, but

  be ready to start small (Job 8:7)

- You must have something. David a sling, Moses had a?

- How much do you have in savings now?

How to raise funds for your Business

- You can raise funds for your business through:

- Family

- Friends

- Investors

- Sponsors

- What skills can you sell to generate emergency money?

- Is your idea marketable enough that investors can come in?

PLEASE DON'T EVER CONSIDER LOAN AS A WAY TO RAISE FUNDS FOR YOUR BUSINESS. WHY?

- It's a new business; it may not run as it is in your paper.

- Environmental situations such as flood, excessive rain can also affect your business. Availability of resources on time also could affect.

- If you borrow money to run your business, you are no longer on your own, but you are working for your creditor!!!

- **Avoid high blood pressure, hypertension – stay away from loan!!!**

Why start –up Businesses fail

- Starting or going without God

- Poor execution of plan

- No viable market

- Undercapitalizing the business- removing money from the business to solve personal needs.

- Picking a niche that is too small

- Competing head to head with industry leaders

Businesses to start with little capital

There are a lot of businesses you can start with a little capital. Some are listed below:

1. Printing Jobs

2. Snail Business

3. Selling Liquid Soap

4. Digital Marketing

5. Nigeria movie industry: Do you know that there is a lot of money in the Nigeria movies industry
   - Script Writing

- Story – Contact producers, don't sell a story, instead ask for a role in the film that will earn you more.
- Film screening – Call producers during festive period and offer them a space in return for a percentage after the event.

6.   Making money from Nigerian millionaires: You can do this by providing supporting services such as making portraits of them. There will be a point in your life. When somebody will ask you, "What can I do for you?", what will you ask for? (A) Money (B) Mentorship (C) Job. Don't plan on what somebody will give you tomorrow – it is only God that can help.

7.   Writing Biography: Writing a biography about millionaires is one of the ways you can raise money for yourself.

8.   Exportation Business: It is very lucrative. E.g Milo, sugar, pepper, ogbono, egusi, smoked fish, natural honey, kolanut, seasoning, pumpkin leaves, crayfish, dry smoked snails, Ribena, peak crown milk, Nigeria home video, Nigeria daily news paper.

9.   Event planning: Organise an event that will connect the high and mighty. Organize competitions. It can be started with N25,000. Every company must have an event. Look for one good event.

10.   Writing children stories in dailies.

11. Help Nigerians set up Non-Governmental Organisations(NGOs). You need good people as your board members. Board members determine how far the NGO can go. You can also affiliate with

international NGOs. Check out their website, send them mails that you want them to be in Nigeria.

IN SUMMARY

Life after NYSC

Criteria for a Job

- Skilled: You must be skilled in your area of specialization.

- Team spirit

- Readiness to work

- Ability to learn quickly ...

- Necessary qualifications

- Marketable CV

Things to remember about successful entrepreneurship

- Successful entrepreneurship starts and ends with God.

- Know yourself- locate your passion

- Have the right motive – money should be the last

- Find a problem people are struggling with and solve it profitably.

You can download sample business plans on

www.okemscube.com/business-plan-downloads

About Okemscube

Okemscube Multiventures is an ICT company founded in April 2012 by a then serving corps member.

She has long passed out, but she is passionate about corps members achieving the best of their service year.

One of the ways proposed to achieve this is through adequate training relevant to each corps members need.

At Okemscube, we believe in Empowerment of Nigerians especially Youths in emerging technology practices to achieve financial buoyancy.

Our Services are:

I. Professional & Technological Based Training

- Basic computer training.
- Diploma in web development.
- Certified web programming.
- Project management professional.
- Hysys
- AutoCAD
- Online Business Management
- Comptia A+
- Comptia N+

Any course you want, we will get it for you.

II. Bulk Sms - www.smsnbusiness.com

III. Web Design Complete Package

- Web Design & Development
- Web Hosting - www.justhostng.com
- Domain name registration

IV. Business centre services

- Cyber Café
- Graphics design
- Information Marketing
- Online business management
  www.onlinebiz4real.com

V. ICT Consultancy

- Supplies of computers & ICT Equipment
- Business solutions with IT deployment
- Computer Engineering & Repairs
- Event / Project Management

VI. Entrepreneurship Development

- Registration/Incorporation of business
- CBN-NYSC awards for business proposal
- Business plan writing

We would like to hear from you.

info@okemscube.com

www.okemscube.com

08053947352, 08063250637

At Okemscube, we provide Quality Education and Services.

Suite 1, 2nd floor, DeinjoyPlaza by Oguruguru Native Pot, 55, Erepa Road, Yenizue-Gene, Yenagoa, Bayelsa State

BONUS

For purchasing this book, download our latest book at our store, send SMS from your phone to 07055333000

In the format

bookjob +First name+last name +Email Address + location

e.g

bookjob + olukemi +oyeleke + olukemi@okemscube.com

Or log on to www.onlinebiz4real.com/bookjob

www.ingramcontent.com/pod-product-compliance
Lightning Source LLC
Chambersburg PA
CBHW070552160726
48003CB00005B/2019